The New Moonlighting

How to find work and make money on the Internet freelance job market

by Bob Cohen

The New Moonlighting

By Bob Cohen

bobology

11278 Los Alamitos Blvd., #204

Los Alamitos, CA 90720

bobology.com

First Printing April 2014

The Internet Marketplace

What is the Internet Workplace?

The new Internet Marketplace consists of websites and smartphone apps that connect people who want to buy services and products with the people that can provide them. The website or app provides a convenient place for buyers to locate services and products with the capabilities of a website or app. The websites and apps of Internet Marketplace essentially act as brokers, bringing buyers and sellers together, and in many cases these websites and apps may handle the transaction. Sometimes the marketplace is a website, sometimes a smartphone app, and sometimes both, so you'll see me refer to them as websites and apps.

Specialization

Internet Marketplace websites and apps specialize in specific types of services and products, helping both buyers and sellers reach each other. For example, one website, AirBnB, is focused on helping people rent rooms and places to stay to travelers who want alternatives to hotels. Another marketplace app, called Task Rabbit, helps connect locals who need tasks and odd jobs (cleaning, delivery, repair, or organizing) to others who can do them.

Benefit to the Buyer

The focus on specialization is what makes these Internet Marketplace websites and apps so effective.. By using the Internet, sellers can find customers and things easier, and sellers can reach people who want their services or products. There's a market for buyers who prefer to deal directly with individuals rather than a company or a business, and they search for individuals who provide personal attention and customer satisfaction.

By using a third-party website or app to act as a go-between, buyers can often see reviews and ratings, which assure them of a high level of quality for the service or product they purchase.

Benefit to the Seller

Sellers of services and products find the Internet Marketplace beneficial because these websites and apps help them find new customers, make it easy to obtain repeat customers, provide an Internet location for their work, set prices, and collect money when the work is completed or delivered. For anyone looking to do work for someone else, these websites and apps almost eliminate the risk of not being paid. Buyers send their payments to a website or app, which then sends the money to the seller. No money exchanges hands directly, and both the buyer and seller are protected by the contract terms provided by the website or app.

The honest answer is that it all depends on your skills, resources, product, location, and how much you're willing to work. Since these websites are now marketplaces, other people offer services and products, and marketplaces allow the price to be set based on supply and demand.

Some people make $200 an hour for their skills and expertise— others make a few extra dollars selling handmade items on Etsy. Others make $5 for a service on sites like fiverr, while others are making $50,000 a year on Etsy. People even make five-figure incomes renting their cars. The demand for what you offer will determine its worth, so higher-demand skills and products will generate the most money. But regardless of what you offer, you can always help yourself by being a good entrepreneur.

Entrepreneurship versus Employee

While government employment laws determine whether a person is an employee or an independent contractor, from your point of view, the difference amounts to how you're paid. An employee is paid a wage or salary, while an independent contractor is paid for a task or assignment. You'll see terms like "independent contractor," "freelancer," and "entrepreneur" used interchangeably to refer to work that is contracted, rather than paid with a paycheck. As an independent contractor you are considered self-employed, and are responsible for your own expenses and time. You are responsible to deliver a finished product to the person or organization who hires you.

If you've only worked as an employee, becoming a entrepreneur may seem intimidating, but the websites, apps and resources in this book will help make it easier to get started. Many of the websites and apps offer tutorials to help you learn more about being an entrepreneur, setting prices, managing customers, and increasing your income. The websites and apps I mention in this book depend on people like you to deliver quality services and products, since most of them make their money by charging the buyer or seller a small fee for each transaction. Internet marketplace websites and apps succeed when more buyers and sellers use them for conducting business.

As an independent contractor, you are responsible for your own bookkeeping, taxes and expenses. Let's look next at the options you should consider as a business owner .

Organization and Ownership

For most people, sole proprietorship is a good starting point. With a sole proprietorship, you are the owner, do business under your own name and are personally responsible for the business.

Other forms of organization include partnerships, limited liability corporations, S Corporations, and C Corporations. Each type has various tax and legal implications. Consult with an attorney and a tax advisor, accountant, or CPA for additional advice. Good advice is important because each form of organization and ownership has various local, state, and federal reporting requirements.

Fictitious Business Name

If you're doing business under your own name, you don't need to file a Fictitious Business Name (FBN), which is also often called a DBA (for "doing business as"). In California and most states, you file a FBN in the county where your business is located. If you choose to do business under any other name than your personal name, you're required to file and record a FBN. You'll also need a record of the filing in order to open a bank account under the business name and make deposits.

Website

Since you'll probably need a business website, you should also consider registering a domain name.. I've found that a free blog with blogger will more than do the job for a website and it's easy to setup and update. You can set it up at blogger.com. To register a domain name you need to use a service called a domain registrar, such as GoDaddy or Network Solutions. You don't need to have your website and domain name handled by the same company, and you can use your domain name at blogger.

How to Use the Internet Workplace

What to Offer?

Your skills and resources will determine what you can offer for sale on the Internet marketplace, so a good place to start is by making of list of everything you can offer a potential customer.

Skills

The Internet Marketplace helps bring buyers and sellers together. You're the seller, and you need to determine your "product" and how to market it. Create an inventory of your skills, abilities and talents. Don't worry about whether anyone would want them or not at this point. It doesn't matter right now if you've ever been paid for any of these skills, it's just a list so you have an idea of your talents.

Examples could include writing, sewing, babysitting, or computer programming. Keep updating your list. Ask your friends what skills they see as your strongest.

Resources

Make a list of your resources. These include things like a car, truck, house, garage, additional helpers, computers, smartphones, and any other physical possessions you own.

Credentials

Also inventory any credentials you have. A credential is anything that you've obtained from an organization like a school, industry association, or the government. Examples of credentials are diplomas, industry certifications, or licenses.

Services or Products

You can offer a service or a product. A service is something you do for a buyer, while a product is purchased and delivered. Generally, when you perform a task for someone, you provide a service. Clients pay for your time, knowledge and abilities. You deliver products to the buyer. However, products don't have to be physical. For example, a book can be either a hard-cover, paperback or an ebook. It's still a product if it's an ebook, it just doesn't have any physical form. An ebook is an example of a digital product for which the market is very large. Digital products include books, music, software, graphics and more.

Location

Think about how far you are willing to travel to work for others. You don't want to travel just to obtain work, since it may not make any money for you after you pay for gas. But think about where you would travel anyway, because the new location might present new work opportunities.

Time

What hours are you available to work? How much time can you spend traveling? Do you have other obligations that might interfere with your assignments? Your reputation depends on treating every customer as though they are a reference, so avoid overcommitting. Be sure you complete every task or assignment when it's due or when you committed to complete it to maintain your reputation.

Getting Started

As we go through different types of buying and selling opportunities, you'll discover services you can offer and the websites and apps to help you find buyers. Once you identify a website or app that appeals to you, register on the site and complete a profile.

Registration and Application

Registration requires that you have access to a computer, the Internet, and an email address. In some cases you'll need a smartphone, particularly if an app is required.

Your Email Address

Your email address says a lot about you. People make assumptions about others based on their appearance and clothes. They also make assumptions about you from your email address and your email provider. People assume anyone with a gmail.com email address is more tech-savvy than any other email address, while a yahoo.com address is close behind. An email with AOL means you're older, and one with a local Internet service like Verizon or AT&T reveals you didn't know how to get a better email address. Like it or not, these are assumptions made by Internet users, so don't let them get in your way.

Google's and Yahoo's email accounts are free, so if you don't have one, sign up for one. You don't need one if you already have your own domain email address (usually provided by your website hosting service). In my case, I have a website with the domain name of bobology.com and my email address uses my name, then the @ sign for my email - @bobology.com. A domain name email address is useful if you want to give the impression you are an established entrepreneur or business, otherwise Google and Yahoo are more than sufficient.

It's also important to use a separate email for any moonlighting you might be doing independently of any other occupation or employment.

Assessment

Depending on the Internet marketplace website or app, you may have to complete a skills assessment test or provide documentation as proof of your identify or of a credential. Part of this process determines if you understand and can use the website or app to accept and complete tasks, so it's a screening tool for the website and the buyers.

Skills assessments are generally used for computer and language skills, and are done online. The website or app requires you to complete a task and submit the work for review. Don't rush through this! Your first assessment will determine your skill level, affect the jobs you are offered, and the rates you can charge.

Be prepared to scan documents required for submission. If you don't have a scanner, find a friend with a scanner or visit a copy shop.

As a condition of being accepted on a website or app for work, you may have to agree to a background check or provide a fingerprint scan. Some websites require pre-employment checks not only to test your skills, but also for insurance or as selling feature to buyers who want licensed contractors.

Creating a Profile

A profile is a description of you and your abilities, talents, and capabilities. Here is where you "sell" yourself, but be honest. Internet users will see your grammar, photos and work portfolio. If you can afford it, get a portrait photo from a professional photographer and wear attire appropriate for the work you'll be doing. Business casual is OK for most anything.

Ratings and Recommendations

Once you have a profile on any Internet marketplace website or app, you'll want to get a recommendation or rating as quickly as possible. To do this, you need to have a customer or perform a task. In some cases, only authorized buyers are allowed to create ratings and reviews. Do some work first. If the Internet marketplace website or app doesn't ask the buyer to review you, reach out to them and ask them to provide one. If the website or app allows anyone to use your services or buy your products, ask one of your friends or family members to buy from you and write a review or rating.

Ratings and reviews help reduce the buyer's risk in using an unknown service or product. Think of Yelp and the impact the site has had on local businesses. People who receive higher ratings and reviews can increase rates for their services and the higher ratings may give you access to better paying work.

Services

Freelance Work of All Types

Types of Freelance Work Done On the Internet

Sometimes it's more cost-effective for companies to hire freelancers (rather than employing in-house teams) for certain types of work. Web development, marketing, SEO, content writing, programming and data entry are just some of the types of work that can be outsourced to freelance workers. Websites for freelancers are a great way for companies to hire freelancers, and for freelancers to find work. The hiring organization can outsource one-of and one-time tasks completed by experts from around the world, using a freelance website to locate and find people with the skills and capabilities they need. Organizations save money and time while freelancers find good employment opportunities.

How These Sites Hire Freelance Workers

Various websites like elance.com, freelancer.com and odesk.com allow employers to post jobs online. The hiring organization registers on the website and then posts jobs, including payment details. Websites like elance.com allow freelancers to pitch for the job allowing the hiring organization to choose a freelancer by reviewing their profiles. Suitable freelancers may also be found using the search option on websites like freelancer.com based on job category, country, hourly rate, ratings and so on.

On sites like fiverr.com, organizations cannot post jobs, but can browse through services offered by various freelancers. If someone likes the offer, he or she can order it. The work will be completed by the chosen freelancer. The client pays only when he or she is satisfied with the work. The freelance sites handle the invoicing, taxing and delivery of payment.

Telecommuting Jobs

While this book is focused on entrepreneurship, you'll also find opportunities for part-time flexible work as an employee, rather than a freelance contractor. An organization may prefer that work be done by an employee rather than an independent contractor. In these cases, the jobs are called telecommuting or flexible jobs. There are a number of reasons an organization may want to use an in-house employee so let's look at a few.

An organization may need to comply with state or federal regulations. The nature of the assignment, such as being available at specific work hours or locations, may require the organization to classify the work must be done by an employee rather than a contractor.

Some work may require specific training requirements that workers need to complete before they are considered trained. An organization wants to make sure that potential employees commit time and effort going through training.

Other work may require access to confidential information.A a result, they hire employees and ask for a specific commitment of time so that the employee doesn't take on work from a competitor.

And there are some types of work where the employer might supply expensive materials, office equipment, tools, or other resources, which can be insured if they are used only by employees. They might feel more comfortable with providing these tools to employees rather than contractors.

These are just a few reasons that an organization might use an employee instead of a freelancer or contractor. The website flexjobs.com lists telecommuting jobs in addition to freelance work.

Websites for Freelance Work

- flexjobs.com
- freelancer.com
- elance.com
- odesk.com
- fiverr.com
- mturk.com

Babysitting

An Overview of Online Babysitting

Babysitting websites connect nannies, babysitters and caregivers with families and individuals with kids. These sites make looking for qualified caregivers easy and convenient. So whether you are a work-at-home parent who needs help with your toddler, a full-time working professional with little time to assist your teens with homework or a freelance babysitter, babysitting connection websites can be very useful.

How Families Can Use Babysitting Sites?

If you want to hire a nanny or babysitter, sign up with the site in question. Once you've registered, you can post your job. Responses trickle in quickly, and you can proceed to check out candidate profiles and request background checks. The last step is to interview the selected candidates before making the final hiring decision.

Some websites offer membership packages where a basic free membership provides you a partial view of caregiver profiles and permission to post limited jobs. Premium packages offer a choice of monthly rates. SitterCity, for instance, currently offers three plans: a \$35 monthly membership, a \$70 three month membership and a \$140 yearly membership. You can post unlimited jobs, read parent reviews, run background checks on freelance babysitters and more.

Some websites like Care.com allow you to post job ads and view applicants' information for free, but you'll pay for a membership to contact babysitters directly.

Online babysitting sites allow you to conduct a quick, targeted search by providing a drop-down menu of caregivers' experience, age, education and other details. You can access a considerable community of caregivers in your area catering to different requirements,from special needs and infant care to assisting with homework and working with teens. You can make one-time payments to caregivers through the site by using your credit or debit card (these are typically the only modes of payment allowed).

You will find baby sitting websites exclusive to one country or connecting caregivers and care-seekers across different countries. If you wish to try a babysitting site, quite a few that offer this option, including SitterCity.

What Caregivers Must Know

As a babysitter looking for part-time work, you can advertise your services on most babysitting sites by signing up for free. You will need to provide pertinent details, which will be verified before you can create your account. Verifying the authenticity of freelance and full-time babysitters allows sites to ensure safety to parents using caregiver services. showcase your abilities in the best possible way.

To showcase your abilities, take time in answering the open and close ended questions (which can be quite exhausting, but be patient and complete this step). Sites may charge a fee for background checks, since there is a cost involved for this step. Some sites offer subscription packages to feature your profile, which may help you to promote your services. Some websites even offer additional features like a weekly calendar of availability so parents and babysitters are on the same page.

Payments are made through the site via debit and credit card by the buyer and sent to you from the website. Tools for calculating care costs can help caregivers understand how much to charge for full-or part-time work.

Babysitting Websites

- sittercity.com
- care.com

Technical Work

Find or Provide Technical Work in Your City

With the growing reach of technology, the demand for technology jobs has increased. Whether you're seeking technology or engineering jobs or providing services, you can use the help of websites that connect service providers with consumers, like onforce.com, sologig.com and installs.com. Connecting technical professionals and IT experts with companies and individuals looking for part-or full-time support, these websites provide a host of services that benefit both parties.

How Companies Hire Freelancers

Technical websites allow companies, organizations, and individuals to advertise projects for freelancers. These websites help connect buyers who need technical skills with ideal candidates and help them specify certain task requirements such as project expectations and pay scale. These websites offer a wide and proactive resume database organized by skill and experience to make the search for a freelancer simpler, faster and more effective.

For organizations who need technical professionals for regular assignments, this technical job websites can help companies create an online presence through job branding. With a targeted approach to finding employees, technical websites can help an organization directly contact professionals who are experienced and skilled in the relevant fields.

Benefits for IT Professionals

If you are looking for freelance IT jobs, part-time, or even full-time temporary work, technical websites can connect you with different companies across many cities and states. Professionals can find jobs according to their expertise and specialization, and these websites use a searchable database to find a relevant list of potential employment opportunities. Since many organizations need technical professionals an an "on-call" basis, there are options for professionals to setup text and email alerts for assignments.

The website pays you, and some customers have requirements to complete specific paperwork before releasing payment, so be sure to complete any required documentation and any required signatures for the assignment. The customer or the website often verifies the work and contacts the customer to make sure the assignment was completed, so you might be rated based on this feedback.

Since there are many industry certification programs for technical professionals, these websites often ask for or require proof of certification before accepting a technical professional on their website. However, many types of technical skills don't have any specific credential, and your experience may be adequate, so don't let the certification requirement discourage you from this work.

In case you're wondering, many large and well-known brand names use these types of websites to arrange and contract for on-site field technical work, including Dell, Cisco, and others.

It's difficult for a product manufacturer to maintain a full-time field technical staff when they don't know how when and where they need to send people, and developing a good reputation can lead to some lucrative assignments on these site.

Technical Work Websites

- onforce.com
- installs.com

Cleaning Services

Connect With Cleaning Services Online

Maintaining the upkeep of your home or office is an important task, best handled by professionals. Many websites feature professional cleaning services and connect them with individuals as well as organizations looking for one-time or contractual cleaning services. These websites contain and manage databases of cleaners organized by location and price, allowing customers to choose the right service for their budget.

How Customers Can Find Services

Websites offering cleaning services include information on service providers and catalog them by state, city, neighborhood and price. By selecting these categories, customers can search for part- or full-time cleaning services. The cleaning services listed on such websites are also categorized by the nature of cleaning, such as residential, commercial or industrial.

Those searching for cleaning help can even specify the number of persons needed, ideal timing, and other job requirements. Some of the websites offer the ability to mark a service provider as a favorite, so you can easily locate them for future work assignments.

Opportunities for Making Money

Websites listing cleaning services in an organized manner create great opportunities for both individuals and established cleaning businesses. You post your profile details on the website including your price range, types of services, and schedule. These websites also allow you to create an attractive profile by listing your credentials, experience, and any special capabilities. Whether you are a small or large company, maintaining online visibility can boost your cleaning business as more people turn to the Internet to find services.

Customer ratings and reviews from satisfied customers are listed with each provider's profile, making it easier for customers to find the cleaners with the highest ratings, so be sure to ask for ratings and recommendations from each assignment.

- homejoy.com

Dog Sitting

Online Dog Sitting

If you are a pet owner preparing for a long vacation away from home, taking care of your pets could be one of your main concerns. A dog sitting website is a great way to connect pet owners with potential pet sitters. These websites allow owners to choose local pet sitters based on their neighborhood, making it easy to contact professionals on short notice.

How Dog Owners Use Online Dog Sitting

Dog sitting websites like dogvacay.com provide an easy way to connect with experienced dog sitters.. By adding city, state and neighborhood details in a search, you can get a list of potential pet sitters. These websites also organize your search based on schedule and pay. With a fixed minimum per night rate, you can reserve a dog sitter for a predetermined number of days. Additionally, dog sitting websites provide related services like free pet insurance, daily photo updates, and customer support.

With simple and easy online booking, you can reduce the costs spent on kennels by over 50 percent and rest assured that your pet is in safe hands. Even in your absence, with personal attention, organized schedule and daily care, your dog can continue living in your home safely.

What Dog Sitters Should Consider

Dog sitting websites are open to individuals looking to find work as dog sitters. With safe and convenient online booking, dog sitters are simply required to create their profile, add details and credentials and set a price range for their services. These websites also help create attractive profiles to capture the interest of the pet owners while promoting complementary services like dog grooming and dog walking. One-hundred percent secure payment methods are used to transfer money from pet owners to professional dog sitters.

Dog Sitting Website

- dogvacay.com

Delivery Services

What are Online Delivery Services?

Online delivery services offer courier services for businesses to ensure that local goods are transferred around the city in time. So customers receive their order, whether food, clothing or other items, sometimes as fast as within one hour, these websites have a special emphasis on urban logistics and a dynamic delivery team.

These websites all need people with reliable transportation to handle the delivery jobs from the businesses that are their customers.

How Customers Use These Websites

Making local online purchases simpler and quicker, consumers can use these sites to choose a store or restaurant of their choice. Ranging from coffee shops, bistros, stationary stores, and gadget shops, these websites cover a wide list of local services. After ordering through these websites, the items are delivered to the given address within an hour, ensuring that local businesses, restaurants and other establishments never miss a delivery. With real-time tracking services and reliable estimated times of arrival, the shipper and consumers can keep track of their order status.

While some delivery websites list the businesses that use their services and help by promoting and marketing the fast delivery service available, other delivery websites stay in the background, and allow the business to provide a quick delivery service as though it was their own people and transportation. Either way, they both need people to do the delivery.

How Businesses Can Benefit

Apart from offering professional and timely services to consumers, these websites offer advantages for local businesses. Especially viable for start-ups with limited budgets, these services can help them deliver goods on time.

How to Find Work on Delivery Sites

Those interested in providing the delivery can apply on these websites. The minimum age to join the effective delivery service system is 18 years and candidates with a vehicle and a smartphone are highly preferred. The delivery service you would provide includes picking up the item or product at the specified location and delivering it to the buyer, usually immediately after the pickup.

These delivery services foster a uniquely dynamic team of deliverers who pick up and deliver all types of goods. When a customer places an order with a store or restaurant, the website matches a nearby delivery contractor that can purchase and deliver the order. What makes this delivery service convenient is that the deliverers are allowed to choose their work timing and cities, and they receive hourly wages and tips.

Delivery Service Websites

- postmates.com
- deliv.co

Ridesharing

What is Online Ridesharing?

Ridesharing apps and websites connect people who want to share rides or carpool. Ridesharing is an excellent way for people to get around and be eco-friendly at the same time. It is also convenient for those who cannot drive or who live in rural areas. However, it can be difficult to find drivers who may be willing to give you a ride in their vehicles at a short notice. Ridesharing apps and websites connect you with drivers who are in the vicinity and who can pick you up in a short span of time.

How can Passengers Use Ridesharing Apps and Websites?

Ridesharing apps are more popular than the websites as they can easily track the user's location with smartphones. You will have to download the ridesharing app on your smartphone and register with your personal details, address and credit card information. When you request a ride, the app will either use the address given by you or the GPS locater on your phone to find rideshare drivers who are close by and willing to take you to your destination.

Uber.com tracks passengers using GPS locators on their phones and even sends text alerts to passengers informing their driver's arrival. You can get the fare of the ride by entering the starting and ending points. The amount will be charged on your card and you will receive a payment confirmation via email. Prices vary depending on the place and even on the hours but you can save on parking, fuel, insurance and so on without compromising on comfort.

How to Earn Money as a Rideshare Driver?

Ridesharing is an excellent option for those looking for part-time work. You register yourself as a driver on ridesharing websites. Sites like lyft.com perform thorough background checks and even conduct trial rides before allowing a driver to join. Once you have been given the permission to work, you will need to download the app on your phone and use it when you are willing to drive passengers. The apps provide options to let passengers know when you are available to handle a ride, so you won't receive requests when you're busy. You will be paid by the company that runs the website and not the passengers.

Ridesharing Websites and Apps

- lyft.com
- side.cr
- uber.com

Onsite Inspection (AKA Mystery Shopping)

Guide to Online Onsite Inspection

Online onsite inspection websites offer businesses, especially those in the retail industry, a way to to find contract workers to do odd jobs . Such websites eliminate the need for businesses to hire employees and the interaction time required to hire them. Moreover, shifting or onsite inspection apps and websites are a great way for freelance workers to find part-time work that pays well. Even those with full-time jobs or those who prefer to work at home can look for relevant jobs via such apps.

How to Find Jobs Via Online Inspection Apps

Shops, supermarkets and other retail stores are routinely look for people to check their inventory, prices and displays and to do odd jobs like take promotional pictures, set-up signs and so on. If you love freelance work, but do not like monotonous work, you can sign up on shifting or online inspection apps with minimal details. Many apps like EasyShift require no application process. Once you have signed up, you can see jobs offered by local businesses or stores.

Some apps like Gigwalk assign easy "gigs" or shifts to beginners and increase complexity as the workers gain better ratings and experience. Workers get paid via PayPal on an hourly basis and Gigwalk jobs usually pay between $12 and $15 an hour, with the company keeping about 30 percent of the payment, so you'll typically start out with gigs paying about $5-$7 each.

How Stores Can Find People To Do Onsite Inspections

Businesses looking to find freelance workers or shifters can post jobs on the website or the app along with their deadlines. You will have to register your business and a mode of payment beforehand. There is no need to constantly check on the workers as the apps weed out the bad eggs. Once the job is done, you can rate the worker based on his/her work. If you are satisfied, you can approve the shift or the gig and the app will transfer the payment to the worker's PayPal account.

Websites and Apps for Onsite Inspection

- gigwalk.com
- easyshiftapp.com
- marketforceshopper.com

Article Writing and Proofreading

Online Article Writing and Proofreading Jobs

There is a huge demand for online content as most businesses have started focusing on their online presence. Though there is no lack of skilled writers and editors, most businesses prefer not to hire full-time content writers. Online article writing and proofreading websites allow businesses to find qualified writers to create custom content for them,eliminating the time and effort of interviewing and hiring in-house writers.

How Publishers Find Writers and Proofreaders Online

Companies looking for textual content can register their businesses on these platforms. Jobs are posted on the website and the responses trickle in quickly. You can look through the profiles of the candidates and contact them directly for samples before choosing to work with one. After you have received the work on time, you can rate the writer or editor and approve their PayPal payment.

How Can Writers Find Work Online?

Various online platforms like textbroker.com and zerys.com offer freelance writing opportunities. If you are an experienced writer looking for freelance jobs, you can register yourself on any of these platforms. Some websites ask workers to submit their resumes and work samples for display on their profiles. Once you have registered, you can see all the jobs posted online.

On some websites like elance.com, you need to apply for the writing and proofreading jobs on the website. On others, you can contact the client outside of the website. You can even set your hourly expected rates. Your earnings will depend on the quality, experience and type of content. and Clients state how much they are willing to pay, which can vary drastically. On textbroker.com, writers can expect between 0.7 cents per word and about 1.78 cents per word.

Article Writing and Proofreading Websites

- textbroker.com
- skyword.com
- zerys.com
- demandstudios.com

Virtual Assistance

Your Guide to Virtual Assistance

Virtual assistance websites allow clients to get all kinds of assistance, be it technical, creative or administrative, from workers over the Internet. Virtual assistants are basically contractors who work like full-time assistants without being present physically. They are some of the most sought after contractors online and technology has made it very easy for people who prefer to work at home to be of assistance over the Internet.

How People Hire Virtual Assistants Online? (make money?)

As a working professional, wouldn't you rather focus on your core job and activities than completing paperwork, entering data on computers, setting up meetings, making appointments and researching details? You can outsource these jobs to virtual assistants across the world instead of hiring and paying in-house assistants. Some websites like fancyhands.com have teams of virtual assistants that handle client tasks. Monthly plans can cost between $25 and $65 and their virtual assistants can do everything from booking cabs to confirming reservations.

You can assign tasks to virtual assistants from your mobile device or computer and can even contact them over the phone or online, if required. Some websites allow you to connect with a large group of virtual assistants and interview them. Most websites run background checks on their virtual assistants and allow you to look at their past experience.

How to Find wWork as a Virtual Assistant

If you are looking for part-or full-time work as a virtual assistant, you can register on such websites for free. You will have to provide your resume and contact details along with a mode for receiving payment. After the background checks are done, you can advertise on these websites or choose jobs posted by other companies. Earnings depend on the type of job, the type of contract and your experience.

Websites for Virtual Assistants

- fancyhands.com
- elance.com
- freelancer.com
- odesk.com

Tasks and Odd Jobs

What are Online Tasks and Odd Jobs?

Many websites and apps allow people to hire others to do daily tasks. They also help people earn extra cash by completing these simple tasks. Due to reasons like hectic office timings (?) and personal commitments, most people don't have time to finish their daily chores and errands. They can post an everyday task that they would like to get completed by others on such websites. Shopping for groceries, picking up the laundry, walking the dog, fixing cabinets, are just some of the tasks that can be posted and completed via websites that host such jobs.

How Buyers Hire People to do Tasks and Odd Jobs

Completing small jobs is easy for those who work at home or those who prefer part-time work. To get a task done, you can post a job on websites like taskrabbit.com or zoozz.com. First register on the website and then decide how much you want to pay. Most of these websites offer services only in selected cities, but virtual tasks can be completed by anyone from anywhere. Once you have posted a job, you can review available candidates in the area or allow the website to find an ideal candidate.

After you are satisfied with the completed task, you can pay via various payment modes on the website. TaskRabbit takes a 20 percent commission and if you like working with a particular person, you can request to hire him/her directly.

How to Earn Money Doing Odd Jobs?

If you want to earn extra cash by doing simple tasks for others, register with various websites and create your profile. The website will notify you about the tasks if you are chosen by those who post the jobs. If you like the job, you can accept it and complete it within the deadline. If the client is satisfied with your work, payment will be credited to your account in a day or two.

Websites and Apps for Tasks and Odd Jobs

- taskrabbit.com
- zoozzworkforce.com

Transcribing Video and Audio

Online Video and Audio Transcribing

Some businesses wish to reach a global audience with their marketing messages. However, language barriers can impact the effectivity of the content, especially if it is in visual or audio form. This is where transcribing is necessary. The job may not be frequently needed by a business, so hiring full-time transcribers may not be the best option. Luckily, freelance transcribers looking for part-time work can be found online.

How Buyers Use Oniine Transcribers

You can register on the transcribing websites and then post the video or audio clip that needs to be transcribed along with additional details regarding the job. You also need to mention the amount you are willing to pay. You can choose from various profiles and connect with the transcriber of your choice. Once the work has been delivered, you can approve the payment and rate the transcriber based on the quality of the work.

Find Transcribing Work Online

The best way to find work is to join websites that host transcribing jobs. Most of the time, such websites like ubiqus.com and castingwordsworkshop.com either assign work to transcribers without direct contact with the client, or post jobs from various clients from which the transcribers to choose. To begin,you register with the website, post your qualifications and create a profile or fill out the application forms. Afterward, you can view and select the work that is offered.

Work online or offline at your pace. There are usually no fixed hours, which makes freelance transcribing work an excellent option for those who prefer to work at home or part-time. Once you submit the work, it will be reviewed by editors on the website and you will be rated as well as paid accordingly. As your rating increases, you can access higher paying jobs.

Websites for Transcribing Work

- rev.com/freelancers/transcription
- workshop.castingwords.com
- ubiqus.com

Translation Services

Online Translation Services

Online translation service directories are ideal marketplaces for individuals and organizations looking for professional-quality services. Connecting thousands of professional translators as well as translation companies, these websites offer to link clients with service providers for free. Offering an extensive online directory of services, these websites give freelance translators a chance to work with different professionals and organizations in a wide variety of fields including technical, medical, legal and marketing.

Posting and searching for translation jobs on marketplaces has become simpler over the years as more and more professionals are turning to online sources. Online freelance translation services are becoming an effective and emerging service industry, allowing organizations to keep their costs low.

How Websites Can Benefit Freelance Translators

Individual translators or organizations can register on the website and create a free profile to connect with those who need the services. This not only opens up new opportunities to get clients, but also helps you connect with other freelancers in the directory. Some sections of the profile can also be customized to suit specific geo-locations. For instance, if you are targeting translation and interpretation services for clients from the United States, you can choose this option by adding the information to your profile. Customization narrows down the list of prospective clients and shows you a localized search result.

How Can Online Translation Directories Help Translators?

Covering many global languages including Spanish, Italian, French, German, Arabic, Japanese, Mandarin and so on, online translation marketplaces are an easy way to provide and receive services from anywhere in the world. Freelance translators just have to register with the website and categorize their services based on language and pricing. Any individual or organization looking for translation or interpretation services in the same price range and language can directly contact freelance professionals for more details.

Websites for Translators

- proz.com
- translatorscafe.com

Verified Professional Consultant

What are Online Verified Professionals

Getting answers from the experts for professional or technical questions has become easier with online consulting websites. While you can ask questions on many forums and websites,, you may not always receive satisfactory answers in spite of waiting long enough. With professional online consulting, you can be connected with certified experts to solve your queries. With personalized online conversations, these online experts can answer your questions accurately and precisely.

Getting Answers to Your Questions

Online consulting sites like pearl.com can set up one-on-one discussions with verified and experienced professionals. This will not only help you save time on expensive consulting visits, but answer your questions quickly, without any hassles. These websites include professionals ranging from the medical industry, mechanics, electronic experts, computer technicians, real estate agents, to lawyers and so on. By simply posting a question on the site, you are immediately connected to a verified consultant.

Professionals on the websites are selected based on their experience and quality of service. Stringent verification methods are put in place to ensure that the professionals working with consulting websites are certified, experienced and authentic. Instead of asking questions on general forums with less than helpful responses, you can directly chat with an expert who can guide you on dealing with the situation.

How These Site Benefit Professional Consultants

With a simple registration process, verified professionals like IT experts, beauticians, doctors and so on can share their knowledge, help people and get paid. Online consulting websites allow you to work at any time, from any location.

When you wish to address questions directed at your area of expertise, the website connects you to people asking the questions. You can then choose to answer the question. After the consultation, the client can go ahead with the payment.

Website for Verified Professionals

- ats.pearl.com

Tutoring and Teaching

Learning with the Help of Online Tutors

The increasing influence of the Internet in everyday life is opening up new educational opportunities. Distance learning and online tutorials are becoming easily accessible, making online teaching a practical and beneficial option. Several websites offer students the opportunity to learn from online tutoring on various subjects and levels. Ranging from middle school, high school and college level studies, several subjects are taught with interactive online lessons.

How Online Tutoring Works

Students from all over the world can benefit from online tutoring websites like tutor.com, tutorvista.com and instaedu.com that offer lessons on a variety of subjects. Designed to be interactive, these tutoring lessons include everything from simulations, assignments, assessments and so on that can make learning effective as well as interesting. A classroom style environment is created on a virtual platform, allowing students to learn any subject. Students can conveniently attend the classes online anytime they want. They can also schedule sessions with a preferred tutor after they register with the website.

With low costs, online interactive tutorials are more affordable and convenient for students. Students need to have access to a computer and a reasonably fast Internet connection to attend online sessions on these websites. Students can contact their preferred tutors 24/7 and work on detailed tests for assessment. With unlimited online tutoring, they can also seek help on homework.

Tutors Can Register Online

Online tutoring websites are ideal for experienced teachers looking for an income boost. Owing to their interactive nature, online tutorials can be very engaging and beneficial to both parties. Through websites that offer one-on-one tutoring, qualified teachers can help students with their academics. What makes these tutoring websites even more beneficial is their strict process of registration, requiring verification of credentials before accepting a tutor who can offer their services. By offering your skills and expertise on these online tutoring websites, you can become an invaluable asset to thousands of students around the world.

Websites for Online Tutoring

- tutor.com
- tutorvista.com
- instaedu.com
- tutapoint.com
- eduboard.com
- teacherspayingteachers.com

Sharing Things

How Sharing "Things" Works

A new type of website has become popular which connects people who have "things" they are willing to share with those who are interested in renting them. Some things, like a house, spare room, car, or specialized tool can be expensive to rent from a traditional business. These new websites help bring the renter and owner together, handling the transaction and offering related services such as marketing and insurance. If you own something that other people want to rent, it's easier to make money when you don't need it yourself. If you like renting directly from people and want a wider variety of choices, these websites make it possible to find many things that people are willing to share, for a fee.

Sharing Places to Stay

Share Your Home and Make Money

Budget holidays are slowly gaining foot in the travel and tourism industry as more people opt for affordable travel and accommodations. Instead of relying on packaged tours and expensive hotels, renting local apartments, rooms, boats and tree-houses in other countries is becoming popular, thanks to home sharing websites. Travel sharing websites offer information about registered homeowners from all over the world. With listings from almost 200 countries, these websites offer homes for all budgets in thousands of cities.

Affordable Renting for Travelers

Travel websites with home sharing or renting options employ stringent methods to verify locations and services offered by the hosts. This vetting (? or what?) allows you to choose from an extensive range of apartments, villas, boathouses, tree-houses and so on in any neighborhood of the city. Based on your personal preferences and travel itinerary, you can find many affordable places to enjoy a homey feel. By simply filling out the details for the city, neighborhood, home type and price range, you can select from many options and directly get in touch with the owner. You can also choose accommodations based on the group size, travel dates and availability.

Hosting Tourists in Your Home

With thousands of tourists looking for an authentic and unique experience in a new country, there are many ways you can make someone's holiday more special. Renting out your home during the holidays is also a great way to boost your income. If you are away for the summer or have an additional real estate space ready for occupation, you can share it with tourists. Just register on a travel home sharing site and fill in the details about your home. This information includes everything from rent, area, location, services, amenities and background on the neighborhood. With direct contact from the traveler, you can easily set up a safe transaction.

Websites for Sharing Places to Stay

- airbnb.com
- homeaway.com

Online Car Sharing

For most people, owning a car is either a hassle or unaffordable. If you prefer renting cars and taxis to get around the city, you can rent any of the large number of privately-owned vehicles. Websites that connect car owners with prospective renters are increasing by the day and are proving to be a safe as well as convenient method for both the parties.

Apart from your computer, the services offered by these websites can also be accessed by your iPhone or Android device. Everything ranging from the eco-friendly cars to the stylish sedans can be found on these websites. With a collection of over 1,000 unique models, renting cars online has become cheaper and safer.

Rent a Private Car

To rent a privately owned vehicle, sign up with the website for free and have your credit card and driver's license verified. You can literally rent a car in less than a minute. After you have been approved, you can choose from thousands of cars in your neighborhood on an hourly or daily basis. These websites also provide 24/7 roadside assistance and complete insurance coverage to keep you and the owner safe. You can get these services and more without any registration or annual fees.

Share Your Car

If you have a car that you barely use, renting it out to trusted neighbors can be financially helpful. Within a year, you can earn up to $10,000 even if you rent your car only 25 percent of the time. These websites also have strict screening processes. Choosing safe, experienced and verified drivers, they ensure that your vehicle is in safe hands. Additionally, these host sites provide regular tech support and track the real-time location of your vehicle.

Websites and Apps for Sharing Cars

- relayrides.com
- getaround.com

Reserve Parking Spaces Online

One of the biggest menaces of modern day retail is the pain of parking. With increasing number of vehicles, finding parking space in any big city restaurant, mall or other establishment has become a long and arduous process. The Internet, however, has a great solution to put parking troubles at bay. Many websites with online shared parking services are fast emerging, allowing commuters to reserve a parking space at a busy airport or other location. Whether you are heading out for dinner or a movie, you can now drive without worry with a reserved parking space.

Finding and Reserving Parking

Online parking reservation websites have extensive directories with locations, pricing and availability along with real-time updates that you can access on your computer and phone. By reserving a parking space online, you also learn about discounts in other garages, parking lots and private parking areas. Additionally, you can rent certain residential driveways and find a safe as well as convenient location to park your car for a few hours. With these helpful services, you not only save time but up to 70 percent of parking expenses. Owing to stringent verification and 24/7 customer support, you can be assured that your car is safe.

Renting Out Your Inventory

What sets these websites apart is that you don't have to own a large garage or parking space to register. You can earn extra cash even if you have a single car driveway in your home. It all depends on the need for parking in a location whether people. A driveway or parking spot near a convention center, beach, or busy location is often hard to find and can earn money if you have one available.

Whether you have a few empty spots in your building or own a large garage, setting up a profile on these websites is absolutely free. When putting up the ad for your parking space, you can list out essential details including neighborhood, location, timings, price, area and other preferences. You can also adjust your services to suit your schedule and change your terms and conditions as frequently as you need.

Website and App for Sharing Parking

- parkingpanda.com

Physical Products

Original Designs

Original Designs Online

When you are bound by time constraints, it can be difficult to search for talented artisans and creative designers. At such times, you can find help from several websites that can connect you with artists. With the intention of supporting independent artisans and helping them make a fair amount of money for their designs, these websites help them earn 100 percent of the income. You can connect with several designers and get ahold of rare, cultural artifacts and design pieces at affordable prices without the presence of a middleman.

Purchasing Artistic Items Online

If you are looking for authentic cultural art pieces from local artisans, the best place to search for them is not souvenir shops, but online stores. Connecting you directly with the artisans and craftsmen, you can pay these artists directly. As an art lover, you will also find a greater range of artifacts than commercialized stores and can buy original work directly from local artists. These websites also help customers purchase their desired items at the right price.

Connecting artisans worldwide, these websites offer a wide range of items including jewelry, apparel, accessories, lifestyle products and home decor.

How Artisans Benefit

Easy to use websites like esty.com and globein.com support talented craftsmen and artisans. By creating an attractive profile on the websites, you can post your designs for sale and price them. To benefit the artists, most of the websites do not charge any commission from the sales and instead ask customers to pay a small additional fee.

By using a website that attracts people looking for original designs or hand-made items, the websites attract a large number of prospective customers, and make it easier to reach customers interested in these types of products, rather than mass-produced items.

Websites for Original Designs

- esty.com
- globein.com

Selling Used Things

Make Money Out of Your Used Possessions

Reduce, reuse, and recycle are three golden words to help build a better environment and what better way to reuse and recycle than selling used items online? Day to day items can be passed on to others when you no longer need them. Whether it is used furniture, old books, gadgets or other knick knacks, online sites that connect sellers and buyers are becoming a boon for bargain hunters.

Benefits to the Buyer

One major advantage of purchasing used items is that you can acquire them for a much cheaper price. These websites are excellent places to hunt for bargains on a wide variety of items. They can be particularly beneficial when you are looking for retro accessories, antique items or a product that is not available in your area. The sites are more like yard sales, but only bigger and better.

Selling Used Items Online

If you are planning on getting rid of clutter and have a few items lying around, don't dispose them off. By advertising your sale on popular used item websites like getyardsale.com, you can easily find a buyer who can still use it. These websites are particularly useful when you relocate and want to cut down on your belongings. Whether they are your old clothes, furniture, books, action figures, or utensils, you can always find a buyer willing to pay for items you don't want.

The seller is required to register on the site and add details of the item to be sold along with its picture and price. These websites offer a secure platform for you to directly connect with the buyer and make the monetary exchange. In fact, most websites even assist in packing and shipping to ensure that the sale goes smoothly.

Websites and Apps for Selling Used Items

- getyardsale.com (yard and garage sale listings)
- alibris.com (books)
- craigslist.com
- ebay.com (anything, especially collectibles)
- amazon.com (anything for sale on Amazon)
- poshmark.com (clothes)
- bookscouter.com (books)
- gazelle.com (gadgets)
- technollo.com (gadgets)

Drop-Shipping

How to Make Money with Drop-Shipping

Drop-shipping is the selling of products to customers from someone else's inventory. Companies called "drop shippers" offer a list of products that can be sold on your website or in a catalog. You do the marketing and order processing, send the order to the drop shipping company.They ship the product from their warehouse directly to the customer.

Drop-shipping is used by many websites since it gives a business the ability to offer a broad range of products, without the need for owning the inventory. The website owner only buys the product when they receive an order. Drop shippers sell at wholesale prices, and the website sells at any retail price they choose. It's possible for almost anyone to get into the business of selling through drop-shipping.

How Customers Use Drop-Shipping

A web customer typically purchases a product on a retail website. The website business then delivers the product to the customer, which is called "fulfillment." When the product arrives at the retail customer's home or business, the shipping label created by the drop shipper has the name, address, and contact information for the retail website. The retail customer may never know how the product was "fulfilled," since the shipping label never shows who actually shipped the product.

Making Money with a Drop-Shipping Business

To make money with drop-shipping, you apply to become a reseller for a drop shipper that offers products and shipping services. Most drop shippers charge a fee, sometimes one-time, sometimes monthly, so it's best to do as much preparation in advance as possible before you start paying the fees. Most drop shippers allow you to browse their inventory so you can see if you'd like to sign-up. Some will even set you up with a website and handle the transactions from your customers, making the selling of their inventory a matter of selecting the products you want to sell.

Remember though that retail profits are pretty slim and you may not have that much profit between your retail price and wholesale price. The customer usually pays shipping, so that's not an expense.

Drop shipping works best if you have a customer list already or think you can build one up pretty quickly. Since your existing customers know and trust you, offering a product you recommend is an easy way to add-on additional revenue, or create a new source online.

Top 3 Websites for Drop Shipping

(from http://dropship-services-review.toptenreviews.com)

- doba.com
- wholesale2b.com
- inventorysource.com

Content Monetization

What is a Content or Information Product?

Content can be delivered in many formats and media. Written content can be published on a website, as well as images, video and audio content. Content is simply information—people will pay for the right content. If you can create information, you may be able to make money from the content itself. Writers have been doing this with books, which are a way for people to pay for written content. But in addition to books, DVDs, videos, and media also require good content.

Formats of Content and Information Products

A content or information product is any form of product that is made from text, sound or visual media. Content and information products can be physical, such as a newspaper, book, magazine, or DVD, or digital, where the product exists as a computer file, website, or online video or audio file that is downloaded or accessed on the Internet.

Content vs. Information Products

While a content product is any kind of content, the term "information product" is used to refer to content that is based on expertise and skills - it's usually not a fictional type of content. You see information products every day, in the form of how-to guides, training videos, and magazines. Information products are used by companies and brands to market their brand, and if the information is valuable enough, say, in a magazine, the information is the product.

Some content provides entertainment, but entertainment products are somewhat speculative in nature. It's hard to know what people want until you create it, and it's subject to the tastes and whims of the marketplace. An information product can be created to fill a need, and if you know something that people need to know, you can create your own information product.

Two Approaches to Making Money with Content

Using Content to Attract Visitors

Making money from advertising, affiliate programs, and selling products or services are all based on visitors who arrive on your website or blog taking action.

These approaches use your website or blog content to attract visitors, and then convert these visits with a click or purchase. In these examples the information is essentially free, given away in order to attract attention to a website destination, where some other action results in making money. If the content or information is the product, how can you make money from the content?

Of course, you have a choice for how to make money from information. If you want to make money from your content with advertising and affiliate programs, you can make your information available for free, use it to generate traffic to a website or blog, then make money from the clicks and referrals.

Internet users will often pay for the same information if it's packaged in different formats, since the packaging makes it convenient. A common example is a blog that's available to read for free, but where the blogger has a book that's also available for purchase. The book can be a compilation of blog posts, but since many people prefer a book to reading and clicking on web articles, they buy the book. Even if you provide free information, *always* give people a way to pay you for it.

Using Content as the Product

To make money from information products, you'll need three things:
1. Information that has value
2. A way to charge for the information
3. Ways to reach the people who want it

Let's look at each of these products and the approaches they offer for making money. The first one is content that has value.

Determining the Value of Information and Content

For information to have value of any kind, it has to fill a need. People buy products of all kinds everyday, and the publishing industry is built on selling people information. For an information product to have value, it needs to:
1. Solve a problem
2. Be hard to find
3. Have a motivated audience looking for it
4. With the means to pay for it
5. And have a way to charge money for it

So, the question is, do you know anything that solves a problem, that's not easy for people to learn about for free, that people are motivated to use and that has a target audience with the means to pay for it? If you do, you have a potential information product.

The Value of Information

Determining if your content has value may require a little market research on your part, but the good news is that you can do Internet searches to see what else people are publishing on the Internet that's similar.

For information to be of value, it has to fill a need. This is required for marketing, so ask yourself, "What problem does my information solve?"

The problem your information solves could be for individuals or for businesses, organizations, or government agencies, since all of them buy information products.

Common examples of problems that *people* have are losing weight, managing relationships, and managing money. There are lots of products for all of these needs, since they are so common and also challenging to solve. Other examples appeal to people who need to past a test (traffic school) or to earn a career certificate.

Organizations and businesses have tasks they need to get taken care of, such as marketing, taxes, employee relations and employee development. If you have a professional background or experience in any occupation, you can develop an information product for businesses and organizations if it fills a need.

Hard to Find

Information that's hard to find has more value than information that's available in many places. If the information you have is only available from you, then you're the only source of that knowledge. This is called "scarcity" in marketing terms. Scarcity means that something is not easily available and has a limited supply, which increases the item's value to buyers.

It's possible to publish many copies of a book, but if the book is about a topic that requires the knowledge of someone whose time is expensive, then the price of the book could be very high. If the information is available freely, say from a library or a website, then it would be hard to convince people they should pay for it. The harder it is to find information you want, the more you're willing to pay for it when you find it, especially it it fills a need.

Motivated Audience

While an information product might fill a need, it may not be something that people are looking for. For example, many people might need to eat healthier food, but some just aren't interested in looking for ways to eat better. The difference is in appealing to the people who know they need to healthier and are looking for ways to help them achieve their goals. While the people who aren't looking for ways to eat better are a potential market, if they aren't looking for ways to do it, they are virtually impossible to reach with any kind of marketing.

It's better to have a product that people search for for already, even of others offer similar products, than it is to try to market a product that people aren't looking to buy.

Means to Pay

Even if you have an information product that fills a need, is scarce, and has a motivated audience looking for it, if they don't have the financial ability to pay for it, you won't succeed. Let's say you have a book that helps people pass a difficult test, like a bar exam (for potential attorneys). If you charge $1,000 for the book, someone has to have $1,000 to pay for it, even if it's the best bar exam preparation book in the world. You can lower your price, but if people don't have the money to pay for your information, you simply can't sell it.

The advice here is not to create an information product that costs too much for the people who would be interested in buying it. This is the reason that businesses create and market luxury products, because they know that people who want luxury products have the money to pay for them.

But if you can make money selling a product for $1.00, then you can appeal to a much wider audience, since many people can afford $1.00. But they still must think your information is worth that much.

Don't be afraid to charge for what you know!

Ways to Charge

Two services that I can recommend for selling products directly on your own website or blog are PayLoadz at payloadz.com and ejunkie at ejunckie.com. Both services host your digital files and are integrated with PayPal. Either of these allow you to create an account, upload your digital product to their website, create a shopping cart for it, and then use their HTML code by copying and pasting it on your website or blog.

In addition to these options, WordPress plugins can be used on any WordPress site (a common software for a website) that make digital downloads and ecommerce possible. One other option, if you want one-stop ecommerce, hosting, website and blog is Square Space at squarespace.com.

Making Money with Blogging

What is a Blog?

A blog is a type of website that published content and keeps track of it in chronological order, like a periodical publication such as a newspaper or magazine. A blog can be about any topic. Some examples include education, public transportation, associations, nonprofits, politics, news, and sports. In fact, there's not a subject I can think of that wouldn't make sense for a blog, and there are millions of blogs on the Internet. They are easy to create websites for one person, and as a result, have become one of the most common type of website in use. So let's explore blogs a little more.

The term blog comes from a combination of web and log, which were combined into the term "blog." Blogs are a type of website, and all websites need to be available on the Internet at all times in order for people using the Internet to find them. Like other websites, blogs are almost always "hosted" by a service that provides both the blogging software and the Internet connection as a combined service. Later in the book I'll give you a list of popular blogging services with both free and paid hosting so you'll know where to start your blog.

As I mentioned. all websites, including blogs, are "hosted" on a computer that has 24-hour access to the Internet. Text, photos and other data are located on the computer where the blog is hosted. Blogs include their own web publishing, design and layout tools, each of which are used with a standard web browser and don't require any programming knowledge or computer software.

Blogs display information in a web browser (Internet Explorer, Firefox, Chrome, Safari, etc.) on a computer. The software that manages the formatting and appearance of websites is called HTML, for HyperText Markup Language. HTML includes instructions that web browsers interpret to display any kind of web page, including a blog.

Blogs also include a built-in database to track information chronologically. Like the journal of a ship captain, a blog is a journal that includes content created by one or more authors. That information doesn't just have to be text, it can be any kind of content that can be displayed or used on the web. With a database, a blog is a kind of website that can be indexed and searched. As a result, a blog is an extremely versatile type of website that's powerful, yet easy to manage and use.

What to Blog About?

If anyone ever asks you for advice, you're an expert. That's who an expert really is, someone who offers advice and information. It's up to the person receiving the advice whether they choose to follow it or not. So what might you be an expert on? It could be a hobby, a skill, an area of a city that you know well, relationships, clothes, cars or whatever.

When you share your advice and knowledge online, you are publishing content, and if people find your content useful, entertaining or of value, you will start to get visits to your blog or website. If people are willing to view your content, you can make money from it, which is also called "monetization." Some common ways people create blogs and monetize them are by writing a blog that focuses on a topic they know well. Some ideas are:

· Expertise on a subject you know

· Opinions and advice

· Reviews

· Location information and news in your area

By creating a blog, you are creating your own web publication and publications can make money, so let's see how this is possible.

Ways to Make Money with a Blog

We have four main ways to make money from blogging: web ads, affiliate programs, paid content and selling products or services with ecommerce. With millions of bloggers on the Internet, you have access to a wide range of resources and tools for generating income from your blog.

If your primary goal is to make money with blogging, think about which of these approaches you might want to pursue, either alone or in a combination. Let's review each of these approaches and see how they work and what you need to do to use them.

Advertising Income

Google AdSense

Blogger makes it easy make money with the world's largest web advertising company, Google. With just a few clicks you can add Google ads to your blog through Google's AdSense program. One reason why Google encourages blogging with a free Blogger account is to make more money from advertising. With more space to place ads (like blogs), Google makes more money from the advertisers who use AdWords to purchase pay-per-click advertising.

When a person uses Google to search for something on the web, they type in a word or phrase. The word or phrase is called a "keyword." Google keeps an index of every website on the Internet and the content in each site. After the keyword is entered and the user clicks on "search," Google produces a search result page. This page includes websites that Google decides are relevant to the user's search along with advertisements, usually small text ads at the top or on the side of the web page. These ads are paid for by advertisers who want their ads to appear when someone types in a specific keyword.

When someone clicks on one of these ads, Google makes money. You get paid when someone clicks on an ad that's displayed by Google on your blog. The click fee is deposited in your account and paid when you reach a minimum amount of revenue, usually $100.

To make $1,000 a month on your blog from web ads would require receiving 20,000 clicks at 5 cents per click. Don't be discouraged though as there are thousands of sites making much more. Google is a multi-billion dollar company because people click on their ads.. Google AdSense is free to anyone with a website, regardless of the traffic and volume. There is no minimum amount of traffic you need to have for your blog and the AdSense program is free to join.

Other Display Ad Programs

In comparison to Google's AdSense, other advertising programs typically require a minimum number of unique daily visitors, starting with about 3,000 per day. Once your blog achieves this milestone, you can approach these other advertising programs.

Banner ads are usually sold through advertising services. Advertisers purchase the ad placement with the services, and the services work publishers (?) (bloggers and websites) to display ads. Banner ad programs typically require sites that have asufficient number of visitors before they consider selling ads from their network.

Some banner ad publishers include:
- Value Click Media   valueclickmedia.com/publishers
- Tribal Fusion   tribalfusion.com
- adMarketplace   admarketplace.com
- Traffic Taxi   traffictaxi.net
- Doubleclick   google.com/doubleclick
- Chitika   chitika.com

Self-Hosted Ads

Some bloggers sell their own advertising space directly to advertisers. I've seen PTA groups use this approach to place a sponsor ad for a month or a year in a gadget or banner and cover the cost of hosting. It's your publication, and if you have a specific niche market appeal, this approach can be effective in making money, particularly with local and small businesses trying to reach a targeted audience. Be sure to draw up a contract for advertising. I recommend collecting payment in advance.

Using Blogger for making your first blog site is the easiest way to start selling ads. Google has an "earnings" link in the settings which will walk you through setting up your AdSense account. There is no minimum traffic for your blog to start publishing Google AdSense ads.

Remember, you make money when Google makes money, which is when people viewing your blog click on the Google ad that appears.If you make it public and searchable, Google searches your website and uses keywords to decide which ads to display. If you have content on cars, you'll see car-related ads, content on finance, finance related ads etc.

You can use your AdSense account on any website or blog. There is no need to create a separate account, but you do need to register any additional websites for Google to index and track the ads.

Affilate Programs

Affiliate programs allow you to refer people to a product, service or other item and get paid when someone buys that item or service ranging from software to books andto home loans. Each have payout fees based on referrals from your website. When you join an affiliate program, you get an account that creates a cookie, and you add the affiliate link (instead of a standard Hypertext Link) to take a reader to a page with a product or service.

You are a "referring" website, and the affiliate company knows the referral came from you because of the tracking cookie that is contained in the affiliate HTML link. I recommend starting with Amazon's affiliate program since it's likely if you've ever bought anything on the web, you've probably bought something from Amazon. Their affiliate program makes it easy to sign up and use. Plus, they offer extensive online help.

Some companies have their own affiliate programs but many businesses use affiliate networks. You enroll in the network and then apply to be an affiliate in each of their sponsor programs. Some advertiser programs automatically accept your application, others require approval and to review your site or blog to see if they want to include you in their network. Usually the review determines if they think your content attracts the appropriate audience.

Visit my website for updates on affiliate programs as they change frequently. Some of the most popular affiliate programs are:

- Amazon affiliates: https://affiliate-program.amazon.com
- Commission Junction: commissionjunction.com
- LinkShare: inkshare.com
- ClickBank: clickbank.com
- Link Connector   linkconnector.com
- Bobology (40% recurring affiliate commission)

Except for Amazon, where the affiliate links are for Amazon products, and my own affiliate program, the ones listed here are organizations that provide affiliate services and bring advertisers and publishers together.

If you're a "go-to" person for information or assistance on any topic, using affiliate programs can help generate income. The greater your web traffic, the greater your affiliate program referrals. Be careful not to oversell, however, because your first priority should be to provide quality content.

Using Affiliate Links

The affiliate advertiser provides a small piece of HTML code for your website or blog. HTML code comes in a variety of formats. Some are text only, and display the product or service name in text. Some affiliate links include an image or picture and some links (what? types of code?) are different sizes and shapes.

For you to use HTML links, simply copy the link and paste it into your blog site or post using the HTML provided by the affiliate program. Try out different HTML code from advertisers and paste it into your practice blog to see how it will appear in a preview.

The next time you write a blog or post a photo of a product, remember to use an affiliate link to generate income from your advice and recommendations.

Your affiliate program will track your statistics, which are usually visible on a reporting screen you can view in your affiliate account. Advertisers and programs vary in how much you have to earn before they send your earnings, money, but usually there is a minimum affiliate income that has to be generated— from $25 to $100—before a check or deposit is made into your account.

Paid Content Creator

Blog Content Creation

Successful approaches to getting paid for your content involve establishing yourself as an active blogger. Creating and posting high-quality, well-written articles and content which generates traffic and an audience. As your content grows, your audience will start to include people who are interested in the topics you write about. They will start recommending your blog to others, which will increase your audience.

At some point, as you become established as an expert about your topic, your audience could include other bloggers, journalists, media industry staff and industry experts. There is a constant demand for fresh content on the web. Search Engine Optimization service providers, businesses and other organizations know that they need to update their websites on a continuous basis, and the larger the company, the more important it is to have frequently updated content.

Businesses of all sizes are becoming more aware of the need for dynamic content. By letting people know you're a blogger and content creator, you will find businesses contacting you to discuss creating blog and social media content.

Selling Products and Services on Your Website or Blog

Since a blog is a website, it's possible to sell your own products and services on your blog. Most blogs don't include a shopping cart or ecommerce function, but it is possible to include these functions within a blog, without the need for an external website or shopping cart. For the most part, commerce solutions are designed to handle physical products, digital products (for download) and services. Here are a few of the most common and simpler approaches for a blogger who wants to sell products and services from their own blog.

PayPal

PayPal, the popular online payment system, offers a free account that enables sellers to accept credit cards and PayPal payments. With PayPal's free account, called PayPal Standard, there's no credit application, no recurring monthly fees and no setup fees. Your product or service descriptions are included on your blog. You setup your products or services as items in your PayPal account. Each item is assigned a "Buy Now" button, and the HTML code for the item is inserted into the blog.

This approach lets the blogger place a product within a blog post, so a reader can purchase an item directly from the post without having to visit another web page. Another approach is to create a web page or pages for products and services, and include the "Buy Now" button link with the items for sale on these pages. Taxes and shipping amounts are set up by you in the PayPal account for each item in your store.

In addition to the "Buy Now" button, PayPay provides a subscription button and a donate button for nonprofits to accept donations. When using PayPalwith the free account, a user clicks on the "Buy Now button" and is taken through PayPal's website checkout pages.

An upgrade to a monthly fee, currently starting at $5 per month, allows you to setup pages on your website for checkout **so a customer never leaves your site** (see two paragraphs above-I think it says the same thing) also, why is this a benefit? PayPal provides excellent customer service and support for their plans and is a popular ecommerce solution. PayPal also works with shopping carts, and of course, they work with eBay, who owns PayPal. To sign up for PayPal, go to the business link at https://www.paypal.com/webapps/mpp/merchant, or look for the seller link and select business at paypal.com.

Selling with a Form

Many products and services are best sold on a blog by using a form. A customer enters information in fields you create when you build the form. Within the form you can include options for the customer to select for their purchase. Common options include a radio selection, a check box or a drop-down list of items. These features offer more flexibility and choice for your products or services, but don't make it too difficult for someone to complete the form. Forms provide the ability to collect more data and offer more choices if that's necessary for your ecommerce goals.

Many form websites include an ecommerce function, host the form, and provide the blogger with cut and paste HTML code for embedding the form in their blog or site. Forms can be used to sell products, tickets, take orders, arrange for services and link to virtual goodsForms with ecommerce capabilities are a hosted service and generally require a small monthly or annual fee. Some popular form sites with ecommerce capability are:

- Formstack   formstack.com
- Wufoo   wufoo.com
- Formsite   formsite.com

Booking Appointments Online

Another way to make money is to use an appointment booking service on your website or blog. If you offer services by appointment, using an online booking service, your customers will have the ability to pay for your time and book an appointment from your site or blog.

One of the most commonly used services for this is BookFresh at bookfresh.com. While you're busy doing work, you can automate the appointment setting process, avoid email and telephone tag and fill up your schedule.

If your work depends on booking appointments, one of these services is a worthwhile investment. Most of them will collect payments for you, integrate with smartphones, and allow for recurring bookings.

Websites for Online Booking

- bookfresh.com
- genbook.com
- simplybook.me

Marketplaces for Digital Products

Since you'll keep all of the profit, I recommend selling your digital products on your own site or blog. You can also offer your products for sale on a site that takes a commission. An example would be a Kindle ebook for sale on Amazon. So why would you use a site that is paid by commission? One reason to sell a digital product on an ecommerce site is to make your product available in more places. It's like shelf space in a store. If you sell your product at Target, someone shopping at WalMart would never see it. So if you sell your product on your own website or blog, selling it in other places makes it available to people who may not find your own website or blog.

Websites like Amazon generate a lot of traffic, and many customers have payment information on file with Amazon, so they like to buy things on Amazon because the payment process is fast and easy. But, you might not have a choice to sell a product on your own website, especially with smartphone apps and content.

All apps created for Apple iPhones are sold through the Apple App Store, while Google Android apps are sold through the Google Play app store. There isn't another way to sell an app for smartphones, since they are all installed through these stores. Apple has paid out over $16 billion to app developers, most of whom are entrepreneurs.

However, the stores make it easy for people to purchase and download your apps. And in addition to selling apps for smartphone through Apple and Google, you can also sell music, videos, and ebooks in their online stores. You can promote your smartphone digital products on your own website or blog and link to your product on the Apple and Google stores for people to buy them.

Digital Product Stores

While there are many places to sell digital products online, in this section I'll cover some of the most common ones.

eBooks

Amazon is the number one website for selling ebooks, and books sold on Amazon are in the Kindle format. Since there are tens of millions of Kindle readers, so people think of Kindle as the number one place to go for an ebook. Other sites sell ebooks such as Apple's iBook Store and the Google Play Bookstore. You're free to sell your book on as many sites as you wish, including your own website or blog. If you aren't sure how to publish an ebook, there are classes available through community colleges and online. One website, smashwords.com, has extensive how-to information and will publish and list your book on multiple ebook marketplaces for you.

ebook websites:

- Amazon: kdp.amazon.com
- Apple: https://itunesconnect.apple.com/WebObjects/iTunesConnect.woa/wa/iBooksSignup
- Google Play Bookstore https://play.google.com/books/publish/signup#settings
- smashwords.com (publishes your book to ebook stores)

Music Websites

- Amazon Createspace: https://www.createspace.com/Products/MP3/
- iTunes:.apple.com/itunes/working-itunes/sell-content/music-faq.html
- Google Play: https://play.google.com/artists/
- CD Baby: cdbaby.com

Photo and Graphic Websites

- bigstockphoto.com
- istockphoto.com
- pond5.com
- fotolia.com
- shutterstock.com

Training Video Websites

- Udemy: udemy.com
- Amazon Createspace: https://www.createspace.com/Products/DVD/

Additional Ways to Make Money with Information

If you have information that people are interested in and build an audience, there are some additional ways to make money from your content, these include sponsorships, paid email newsletters and membership websites. Let's start with sponsorships.

Sponsorships

Sponsors are brands who pay a fee in exchange for promotional consideration. The promotion can consist of an endorsement, product placement, ad or a mention of the product or brand in the content. A sponsorship is usually an agreement or contract between the advertiser, the sponsor, and the owner or producer of the web content. Sponsorship is a form of advertising, but instead of the advertisement being produced and occupying space or time, the advertising is placed within the content itself and includes a mention by the content creator regarding the sponsorship.

Sponsorship allows a sponsor to purchase exclusivity and the endorsement of the website or any other media. Celebrity endorsements are a form or sponsorship you're probably familiar with, and you may have seen products used on television shows, mentioned by radio broadcasters or promoted through other forms of media. If you don't have a television show or radio broadcast, one of the most common ways for a content creator to recognize sponsors is with Podcasts.

What are Podcasts?

A podcast is a radio program that is broadcast over the Internet.

The term, which is short for iPod broadcast, originated in 2004. While the original podcasts were designed for Apple's iPod mobile music player, they work with a wide variety of devices. Imagine being able to listen to your favorite programs whenever and wherever you wish.

You can download podcasts onto a computer or any other device capable of playing music and listen to them at your leisure. Usually a podcast is created using a blog and an audio-hosting service. Some blogging sites likeTypePad.com include audio hosting in their regular fee.

Podcast and Radio Differences

Radio stations play song after song, but when you download a podcast, you're downloading a single prerecorded radio program. Podcasts encompass every type of radio program from talk shows and interviews to documentaries and dramas. Some podcasts are devoted entirely to delivering an hour or two of commercial-free music.

Newer podcasts may also include accompanying videos, so subscribers can watch the host interview guests. Some radio stations like NPR include podcast versions of their radio programs on their websites.

Just like radio shows, most podcasts are episodes in a long-running series instead of standalone programs, and they're released daily, weekly, monthly or on any other schedule. To help listeners download new episodes, most publishers update lists of their episodes when they release a new podcast. Many publishers also provide schedules so listeners can see which episodes are coming up in the next few weeks.

Some podcasts are limited in the number of episodes, much like a television mini-series, compared to a weekly television series. The only rule about podcasting is that there needs to be more than one episode.

What Makes Podcasts So Revolutionary?

Because they're prerecorded, listeners don't need to maintain an Internet connection. They can download the podcast and listen to it on a plane or in the car. Podcasts are distributed over the Internet instead of the radio, so listeners can usually download them from anywhere in the world. Listeners don't have to tune in whenever the program first airs, and they can pause, rewind or skip ahead to listen to podcast segments again and again.

Literary writers are also experimenting with podcasts. Novels are hundreds of pages long, and they can require anywhere from 10 to 50 hours to read out loud. Novel podcasts break books up into manageable chunks. A writer can fit about 20 pages into an hour-long podcast, making the format perfect for a daily commute. Listeners can download shorter podcasts faster than longer ones, so they can spend a few minutes downloading a chapter from a novel podcast rather than a few hours for the entire book. With these options, podcast listeners will never want to listen to radio the old way again.

With millions of people connecting smartphones in their cars and looking for listening material during workouts, savvy marketers are using podcasts to reach new audiences. Using podcasts, brand name advertisers are able to reach people who might not have the time to read an article on the web, but are happy to listen during a commute or workout.

Where Do You Find Podcasts?

The simplest and easiest way to find podcasts is by using an app on a smartphone or tablet. Apple has their own podcast app for iPhones and iPads. Using the app, you can search for podcasts available from the iTunes store where all podcasts are free. Android users can access podcasts using one of the popular apps like the highly-rated Skitcher.

Most podcasts can also be played directly from the original website hosting the podcast. Podcasts are available on most topics and can be educational and entertaining. Try out downloading one of these popular apps to start exploring.

Video Podcasts

A podcast traditionally has been audio only, but with improved video hosting resources including YouTube, a video podcast is as easy to create as a YouTube account.

Promotional Consideration

Since good podcasts tend to build up a loyal listener base, many podcasters (the people who record them) arrange to take on a paid sponsor. In exchange for the payment, the podcaster mentions the sponsor one or more times during the podcast. Since the listener is still listening to the voice of the podcaster, the sponsor's message usually is heard, rather than tuned out.

Websites and Resources for Podcasts

- WordPress self hosted - for website
- libsyn.com
- blubrry.com
- Amazon S3 (good for video and audio)
- YouTube.com - for video
- Vimeo.com - for video
- Agreements and contracts: legalzoom.com

Email Newsletter Subscription

An email newsletter is a periodical publication that is sent out using an email software program. The frequency is determined by the publisher, but it's distributed weekly or monthly. Think of an email newsletter as an email format of a magazine.

While many email newsletters are free, and are used to promote a brand or website, some email newsletters are available only by paid subscription. The publisher or author uses a payment service like PayPal, then adds the subscriber to their newsletter.

The key to setting up a paid email subscription newsletter is to use a newsletter subscription service. The primary reasons are that your email newsletters are stored for backup, your email subscription can grow to a virtually unlimited number of subscribers and you won't need to use your personal email account to send out large numbers of emails, which could end up being flagged by your email provider as a spam.

It helps to offer a sample issue for free, then take people to a payment webpage where they can pay for a subscription. Some services like MailChimp and aWeber have connections with payment processing so you can automatically accept payments and add a subscriber to your list.

Email Subscription Services

- aweber.com
- mailchimp.com
- constantcontact.com

Paywalls and Membership Websites

A membership website restricts access to some or all of the web pages to paying members. Often this is called a paywall, since there is an imaginary "wall" which requires payment to pass through by the reader. A paywall is a barrier on a website that prevents visitors from viewing web pages unless the visitor makes a payment. Think of it as the toll-road of web sites. While some roads are free, some roads require a toll in order to use them.

Why Do Paywalls Exist?

While you might think of the Internet as a free resource, someone has to write the articles, take pictures and shoot the videos that we view on the Web. Those people have to be paid to create the content by the people or organization that owns the website. So how do these websites get the money for this? Usually through advertising.

Examples of Paywalls

A regional newspaper, the *Orange County Register*, was purchased by some investors with no experience in the newspaper business. The new owners promptly made the online edition of the newspaper a paywall website and invested in hiring over 350 staff members. Hiring new staff in 2013 is pretty rare in the newspaper business, but the new owners believe that people will pay for better content. Two other newspapers, the *Wall Street Journal* and the *New York Times* are also known for their paywall online editions.

Besides newspapers, many speciality websites charge for their content. These websites typically have some unique or original content that people are willing to pay to access. In fact, my website, bobology.com, is a paywall, with some webpages visitors can access for free and others that require a payment.

Paywall Supported Websites

Some websites have a different approach to making money and charge visitors for viewing the website. When a website wants to restrict access to some or all of it's information, the website uses a paywall. electronic barrier called a paywall. Some of the webpages are free, and these are considered "in front" of the paywall.

Other webpages and content require payment in order to view them and are considered "behind" the paywall. It's up to the owner of the website what is free and what requires payment and how much to charge. As a result, some websites with paywalls give visitors access to some webpages for free while other webpages are behind the paywall.

For example, if a website wanted to make some sample content available, the website may offer access to some articles so visitors can sample the website and try it before they buy it. Other free webpages could include a shopping cart, news or contact information. It's up to each website owner to choose what web pages will be free and which will require a payment to view.

Different Ways Paywalls Work

It's not hard to recognize a paywall—a message usually appears on the webpage letting you know that access to the page is restricted and requires payment. Membership sites and individual articles are the most common web locations using paywalls.

Membership Sites

A membership site requires visitors to pay a monthly or annual member fee in order to access the webpages behind the paywall. With a paid membership, the visitor becomes a member. When visiting the site, members enter their username and password, which then unlocks the webpages behind the paywall.

Some membership sites have more than one level of membership, with tiers at different prices. For example, one level might be $5 per month, while another might be $10 a month. Usually this means that access to additional sections of the website are only available to the higher fee membership level. It's a matter of how much the site owner wants to charge and if the content is valuable enough for people to pay for it.

My own website, bobology.com, is a membership site. Anyone can visit the website and view the webpages that don't require a paid membership to view, but when a visitor clicks on a webpage that is viewable by members only, a message appears on their screen letting them know that the content they are trying to video is restricted to members only. A link is included in the message where the visitor can click and sign up for a membership to access the restricted content.

Individual Pages

The other common type of paywall is the individual article or page type which requires users pay to view a single webpage, such as one featuring an article.. Pay the fee, and then you can read the article. This type of paywall is common with newspapers and publications who sell back-issues and articles, and this type of paywall can also be used with a membership site. If you were going to purchase a certain number of articles, it might be more economical to purchase a membership.

Will Paywalls Become More Common?

Specialty websites with unique information and content have been able to make money by charging and have been using paywalls for many years. If the information is good enough, people using the Internet are willing to pay for it. Most often these sites have been focused on specific industries, occupations, or topics where interested people are willing to pay for the content.

Print magazines and newspapers haven't been the recipients of most of the advertising spending, it's been search websites. So the old idea of supporting a magazine or newspaper with advertising income isn't working for many traditional periodicals. If advertising can't support the business, the creators of content and information will find other ways to make money or go out of business.

Digital magazine subscriptions are available for popular devices like Kindles and iPads, and the subscriptions are usually higher than a subscription to the print edition. While you can find a lot of information on the Internet for free, you're likely to see more paywall websites when you start looking for specialized information or content.

Membership and Paywall Web Hosting

- membergate.com
- kajabiapp.com
- wildapricot.com
- mediapass.com
- WordPress plug-ins:
  - wishlistproducts.com
  - amember.com
  - memberpress.com
  - magicmembers.com
- mediapass.com

Crowdfunding and Donations

How Crowdfunding Works

Crowdfunding is the ability to raise money for a project product or task using a website that allows members to offer money to the project team. Members of a crowdfunding site browse projects that are listed on the site. The members then purchase a "stake" in the project. When a minimum level of funding is reached, the project is "funded," and the money from the purchasers is transferred to the project team. The stake that's purchased varies depending on the type of project, so let's look at some project ideas that appear on crowdfunding sites.

Projects include products that are under development, such as smartphone accessories and electronic gadgets. For a product, the stake is usually a purchase of one of the products when it's available. The purchaser gets early delivery before the product is available to the general public. Other projects are creative, such as a video production, artwork or book. Often a crowd funding site member can purchase a sample of the finished product. is something that a crowdfunding site member can purchase for these types of projects.

Crowdfunding is about support, not just the purchase of a finished movie, book, or product, and as a result there are other types of purchases available on crowdfunding sites.

Many projects offer a range of crowdfunding stakes for purchase. For a movie production, a member might be able to purchase a meeting with the director or producer; for a book, a signed edition form the author; for a game, a special edition with additional features. Crowdfunding is a way for people to make direct offers of support to other individuals or teams.,

Obtaining Crowdfunding Support

Crowdfunding sites differ slightly in their requirements, but all require that you register and provide a description of the project you are seeking to fund. There is usually an approval process, and once completed, your project is listed on the crowd finding site.

Your project description needs a complete explanation, background information, a personal story, along with a video interview of you and your team. Creativity goes a long way in obtaining funding. .

You ask for a specific amount, explain why you need it and what you will do if you obtain the funds, and create levels of support for people to purchase. It's best to offer a range of price points, from $5 and up, and you can see what other projects similar to yours are doing to get an idea of what they offer. You can be creating, offering a personal lunch or access to a film shooting as examples of things to offer crowdfunders. You can also limit the number of offers at specific funding levels to make certain purchases more exclusive.

Crowdfunding has been used successfully by people with an idea, passion, and commitment, and can be used for a few hundred dollars to projects that might need several millions.

Websites for Crowdfunding

- kickstarter.com
- indiegogo.com
- crowdfunder.com
- rockethub.com
- fundable.com
- gofundme.com
- ourcrowd.com
- somolend.com
- appbackr.com
- angelist.com
- quirky.com

Donations

A donation is the difference between requiring people to pay for information and *asking* them to pay for it.

Making Money with Donations for Content

For many years people who created software products made them available for free, and asked for a donation, usually via PayPal. Software developers found that people would not try the software if it required payment.. But if website owners offered their software for free and gave users a choice, many would pay voluntarily because they thought the software was worthwhile. Often the donations are $5 or $10, and software developers who create good software can make some extra money and even a full-time income.

Crowdfunding has helped educate more people about a way to provide donations and contributions for people developing products, media projects and software. The Internet has made it easier for people who need funding to connect with people who are willing to provide support.

Not requiring people to pay might seem like a mistake, but it has proven to be a viable way to earn money from content. In addition to the PayPal donation button approach, a new way for people who create blogs, newsletter, videos and podcasts is with a website called Patreon at patreon.com.

With Patreon, you create an account, then tell people about your project. Members of Patreon (called "patrons"), can browse content providers and pay for each new blog post, video, podcast, etc. whenever a new update is published.

When to Use Patreon versus PayPal

PayPal is good for one-time donations, and works well with an ebook software product, game or any other type of digital download where people would only access it once. Patreon is focused on periodical work. For anyone doing a podcast, blog, videos on YouTube, or a newsletter, Patreon is a way to make your content available for free, while offering people who are willing to pay a way to do so. Often, making money is about giving people a way to pay for what you do, and if it's worthwhile, people will make contributions.

Websites for Donations

- https://www.paypal.com/webapps/mpp/fundraising
- patreon.com

Offline Opportunities

As you learn your way around as a new moonlighter using the Internet Marketplaces I've covered in this book, your own skills and expertise will improve to the point where you may offer services to businesses and organizations. Obviously you can use the general purpose freelancing sites for finding work on the Internet, but there's an additional market, the need for virtually every type of business and organization with a website to communicate with their customers and prospects on the Internet.

With the explosion of websites, blogging, email subscriptions, and social media new types of jobs and contract work have exploded to fill the needs of these organizations. Often, the way to a full-time position is through contract and moonlighting work. But virtually every business and organization knows they should be doing more Internet marketing. Here's a sample of some newer job titles and contract work descriptions:

- Social Media and Blog Posting
- Email Article Writing
- Webinar Production
- YouTube and Video Production
- Podcast Production and Editing
- Developer for Mobile Apps
- Website Designer

I recommend that anyone who does any kind of content creation or uses software tools include that information on a business card or on their LinkedIn profile. You could become more valuable to your current employer, be more valuable to a recruiter, or find freelance opportunities if you let people know you have these skills and expertise.

Additional Websites and Apps

While this book has many ways to make money using the Internet, there are always new websites and apps being released.

Visit bobology.com/thenewmoonlighting for updates on new websites, apps, and other ways to create a moonlighting income for yourself.

11899683R00038

Made in the USA
San Bernardino, CA
02 June 2014